Make Time
for
Reading

A Story Guide
for Parents of Babies
and Young Children

by Jean Ciborowski Fahey, PhD

Illustrated by Peter J. Thornton

Gracey Books
YARMOUTH PORT, MASSACHUSETTS

ISBN 978-0-578-12558-9

Library of Congress Control Number: 2013942095

Book design: Elizabeth DiPalma Design +
edp@edpdesignplus.com

Gracey Books
Yarmouth Port, Massachusetts

Printed in the United States of America
by Universal/Wilde
26 Dartmouth Street
Westwood, Ma. 02090
universalwilde.com

To Shelley
J.C.F.

For Ruth, my first teacher
P.J.T.

THE FRIENDS OF

South Shore Hospital

CARING, COMMITTED,
CONNECTED TO OUR COMMUNITY

This edition was made possible
through the generous contributions of the
Friends of South Shore Hospital,
Weymouth, Massachusetts

ACKNOWLEDGMENTS

So many people have supported me in the development of this book during the past decade. The idea to use a children's story to teach adults was inspired by two women of great distinction: Mary Poplin, my doctoral chair at Claremont University, showed me how to really learn from children. Judy Palfrey, former Chief of Pediatrics at Boston Children's Hospital, took time to read us a children's book at the end of many staff meetings. To both women, thank you so many, many years later.

Two people championed the book from the start: Early childhood expert and author, Betty Bardige and friend and pediatrician, Mike McManus.

And thank you to my parents Dorothy and Chet Ciborowski, Aunt Nat and Uncle Ray Palmer, John, Linda, Colin, and Chris Fahey and his wife Peggy Jameson; and especially Marilyn Cordell, my brilliant creative consultant on call and friends Mary Beth Norris, Gigi Walker, Kathy St. George, Carole Romaine, Peg Hume, Linda Heald, Carol Perkins, Kristi Keinholz and Roseanna Means for their years of support.

I thank my 75 campaign investors, my videographer Alistair Wilson and my friends at the Massachusetts Family Literacy Consortium. Kathy Rodriguez provided comments on the translation for the Spanish version in collaboration with the Student Support and Advising Center at North Shore Community College, the Chelsea Intergenerational Literacy Program and the Worcester Adult Learning Center.

Finally, I acknowledge our dearest daughter Eva, who inspired me to see parenting as an art more than a science, and my Tom, devoted husband and superb writer.

How to use this book

This book will help you learn how to prepare the babies and young children in your life for reading success.

The true story of little Eva will guide you through the science of how children learn to get ready to read.

Read the story on the right pages first. Then go back to the beginning and read the left pages.

Read this book to yourself and to children ...
over and over again.

Make Time for Reading

1. DID YOU KNOW?

Your baby wants to hear you talk, read and sing
in the language of your home and your heart
as soon as she is born.

Once upon a happy time
in a village near the sea,
there lived a child named Eva
and that child belonged to me.

I longed for you to love to read
and yet you were so small.

All the same I'd read to you.
You didn't mind at all!

2. DID YOU KNOW?
Your baby is trying to communicate with you.
Even if you're busy, respond with enthusiasm!

And even though you could not talk,
you'd start a conversation.

I'd chat with you.
You'd make soft sounds —
exchanging information!

3. DID YOU KNOW?

You make your baby very happy when you look into his eyes, massage gently and smile.

You loved it when I rubbed your skin.
"Ooo, ooo," you'd softly coo …

And smiling down upon your face,
I'd coo right back to you.

4. DID YOU KNOW?

If you don't want to read, it's OK to tell stories —
even stories you make up!

Books without words are also fun.

I know you loved your picture books,
but sometimes best of all
were stories I would tell of *you* —
or *me* — when I was small!

5. DID YOU KNOW?

It's important that the people who take care of your baby spend time every day talking and reading .

It made me sad to leave for work. You'd cry and wave "Bye bye."

Then Mrs. Kwong would read to you and soon your eyes were dry.

6. DID YOU KNOW?

When toddlers own a few of their very own books, reading becomes more interesting!

But one fine day at 2 years old
I heard you squeal and shout.
The puppy chewed your favorite book
before I pulled it out!

"NO-NO" you said,
"It's MINE!"

No sniff, no smell, no doggy lick!
Up up on tippy toes …
you reached so high to keep your book
away from Gracey's nose!

7. DID YOU KNOW?

Some children find it hard to sit and listen to a book.
Be patient with your reluctant reader.

Sometimes you'd sit so quietly
until the book was done.
But other times you'd scamper off.
There's Eva, on the run!

I'd wait 'till you were sleepy
and hugging baby sheep …
Then read to you your favorite book
until you fell asleep.

8. DID YOU KNOW?

Children imitate the important people in their lives.
Show them that <u>you</u> read.

And oh — the days the family came
with books to read and keep!

So sweet was Grandma's gentle voice,
but Papa's gruff and deep.

And as for me, I'd read MY books
and look at you to see
that you'd pretend to read yours too,
so you could be like me.

9. DID YOU KNOW?
Playing word games every day will help your child
learn to listen to the sounds of his language,
and later learn to read and spell words.

And then when you were 3 years old you learned that words could rhyme.

At 4 you learned that words have parts — an early reading sign!

So at the store we'd play with words like "**cookie**" "**lookie**" "**me**" …

And "**ap - ple**" … well, it has **2 parts**! and "**ba - na - na**" has **3**!

10. DID YOU KNOW?

Children learn to read through writing.
Give your child lots of time with crayons and paper.

I showed you letters in your book.
To you they looked like squiggles.
I gave you lots of paper then
and watched your pen make wiggles.

Your scribbles soon began to look
a little like some letters.
You made them twist and turn around
and practice made them better!

11. DID YOU KNOW?
The more often you visit the library,
the more wonderful books you can read!

At 5 you learned to print your name.
I was so proud of you!

We set off to our library —
a splendid thing to do!
Your card was such an awesome thing:
it didn't cost a penny.

We borrowed books — some even talked —
and never had too many!

12. DID YOU KNOW?

Daily reading practice — especially in the summertime — will pay off in the school year. Take turns reading and then talk about the story.

First grade began with Mrs. Frank —
your time to learn to read!
But sometimes it was difficult
and you did not succeed.

I watched you sound out letters,
and helped you all I could …
with little words like "cat" and "can"
and harder words like "wood."

You practiced, practiced, practiced …
and some words you forgot.
But as you read and read and read
The easier it got!

13. DID YOU KNOW?

When we help our children learn and love to read,
they will help theirs.

Dear Eva,
I love you, love you, love you.
You are my special one!

My gift to you is reading.
I hope it's always fun.

Read when you are happy,
or when you feel alone.

Please pass this love of
reading on
to children of your own.

Love, Mama

So now you've heard this story —
my favorite tale to tell,
about how children learn to read
and why you read so well!

(the end)

The 13 "Did You Know" Messages by Age Group

INFANT

#1: Your baby wants to hear you talk, read and sing in the language of your home and your heart as soon as she is born.

#2: Your baby is trying to communicate with you. Even if you are busy, respond with enthusiasm!

#3: You make your baby happy when you look into his eyes, massage gently and smile.

TODDLER

#4: If you don't want to read, it's OK to tell stories — even stories you make up! Books without words are also fun.

#5: It's important that the people who take care of your baby spend time every day talking and reading.

#6: When toddlers own a few of their very own books, reading becomes more interesting!

PRESCHOOLER

#7: Some children find it hard to sit and listen to a book. Be patient with your reluctant reader.

#8: Children imitate the important people in their lives. Show them that <u>you</u> read.

#9: Playing word games every day will help your child learn to listen to the sounds of their language and later learn to read and spell <u>words.</u> *

KINDERGARTENER

#10: Children learn to read through writing. Give your child lots of time with crayons and paper.

#11: The more often you visit the library, the more wonderful books you can read!

#12: Daily reading practice — especially in the summer time — will pay off in the school year. Take turns reading pages and then talk about the story.

FIRST GRADER

#13: When we help our children learn and love to read, they will help theirs.

* Parents can easily integrate word games into their day to day experiences. These word games reinforce a child's ability to distinguish 'little' sounds in their language, a critical skill for reading success.

For a demonstration of the word games, view my 8 minute film, **Raising Readers** at www.getreadytoread.org.

For Further Reading . . .

Bachman, Heather J., Carol McDonald Connor and Frederick J. Morrison. *Improving Literacy in America. Guidelines from the Research*, New Haven: Yale University Press, 2005.

Bardige, Betty. *Talk to Me Baby! How You Can Support Young Children's Language Development.* Baltimore: Paul H. Brookes, 2009.

---. *At a Loss For Words: How America is Failing Our Children and What We Can Do About It.* Philadelphia: Temple University Press, 2005.

Bardige, Betty and Marilyn Segal. *Building Literacy With Love.* Washington, D.C.: Zero To Three Press, 2005.

Bloom, Louis, Betty Hart and Todd R. Risley. *Meaningful Differences in the Everyday Experiences of Young American Children.* Baltimore: Brookes Publishing, 1995.

Brazelton, T. Berry. *The Essential Reference: Your Child's Emotional and Behavioral Development.* Cambridge: DeCapo Lifelong Books, 1992.

Dickinson, David K. and Susan B. Neuman, eds. *Handbook of Early Literacy Research*, New York: Guilford Press, 2002.

Hernandez, Donald J. *Double Jeopardy: How Third-Grade Reading Skills and Poverty Influence High School Graduation.* The Annie E. Casey Foundation, 2011.

Knapp-Philo, Joanne and Sharon E. Rosenkoetter, eds. *Learning to Read the World: Language and Literacy In The First Three Years.* Washington D.C.: Zero To Three Press, 2006.

Medina, John. *Brain Rules for Babies: How To Raise A Smart and Happy Child From Zero To Five.* Seattle: Pear Press, 2010.

Shonkoff, Jack P. and Deborah A. Phillips, eds. *From Neurons to Neighborhoods: The Science of Early Childhood Development.* Washington D.C.: National Academy Press, 2000.

Snow, Catherine E., M. Susan Burns and Peg Griffin, eds. *Preventing Reading Difficulties in Young Children.* Committee on the Prevention of Reading Difficulties in Young Children. Washington DC: National Academy Press, 1998.

Wolf, Maryanne. *Proust and the Squid: The Story and Science of the Reading Brain.* New York: Harper Collins, 2007.

Jean Ciborowski Fahey, Early Literacy Specialist, holds a doctorate in education from the Joint PhD Program at San Diego State University and Claremont University. She spent 15 years at a Harvard teaching hospital testing children in reading; served as educational advocate with Boston Center for Homeless Families; authored *Textbooks and the Students Who Can't Read Them;* and produced *Raising Readers,* a film showing on the award-winning web site, **Get Ready To Read**.

She has delivered hundreds of workshops and seminars to thousands of parents, professionals and early childhood educators and appeared on local and national TV and radio programs, including National Public Radio.

Jean also writes a literacy blog: www.journeytowardliteracy.wordpress.com

She lives in Yarmouth Port, Massachusetts, with her husband and daughter. *Make Time for Reading* was inspired by Jean and Tom's daughter Eva, who was born in China and raised to love to read in America.

Peter J. Thornton has been illustrating books for children since graduating from the Rhode Island School of Design in 1978.

Most noteworthy is the popular *Everybody Cooks Rice* series (Carolrhoda Books). Used in elementary schools across the country, this multicultural series teaches students about the diversity of our culture using food as the tool. Also illustrated by Mr. Thornton, *A Natural Man The True Story of John Henry* (Godine), is a "standout retelling" of the classic folk story "John Henry."

When not at the drawing board, Peter can be found around the corner leading a spin class or playing ping-pong at his local YMCA. Peter and his wife Barbara call the Mt. Hope section of Providence home, living in the house next door to where he was born.

The illustrator is very grateful for the support of the following: Carol and the staff of the East Side Mt. Hope YMCA Childcare Center, Rosalind Zhu, Indie Lamb, Leila Hopkins, Amy Punchak, Barbara Thornton, Rosie the retriever from Ryan's Goldens LLC, and Mona Braza from Childs Play RI.